T0014231

MONSTERS & MAGIC OF LANKHMAR

BY MICHAEL CURTIS

Cover Artist: David Griffith • **Editor:** Tim Wadzinski
Interior Artists: Chris Arneson, Jennell Jaquays, Doug Kovacs,
Bradley K. McDevitt, and Stefan Poag
Developer: Chris Doyle • **Layout:** Matt Hildebrand
Publisher & Art Direction: Joseph Goodman

AUTHORIZED BY THE ESTATE OF FRITZ LEIBER

MONSTERS & MAGIC OF LANKHMAR

A SUPPLEMENT FOR FIFTH EDITION FANTASY

FOREWORD

Nehwon, Fritz Leiber, and fantasy roleplaying games are intertwined for me. I first discovered the existence of Nehwon and the fog-shrouded streets of Lankhmar within the pages of *Deities & Demigods*, a supplement released for Advanced Dungeons & Dragons in 1980. Before I perused those pages, I had no inkling of Nehwon's existence or of the fearsome monsters, strange wizards, and dubious heroes that called it home.

It is with great pleasure that I now come full circle on a journey begun over 40 years ago: Nehwon and the original fantasy roleplaying game are united once more. Instead of the young boy who pored over the pages of *Deities & Demigods*, described by James M. Ward and lavishly illustrated by Jennell Jaquays, I'm now the man writing those pages. Hopefully, another young gamer out there is about to discover one of the greatest fantasy settings in both literature and RPGs for the first time.

Fritz Leiber penned more than 40 short stories, novellas, novels, and poems related to Nehwon and the adventures of Fafhrd and the Gray Mouser. It would be unrealistic to assume I can document every magical spell, enchanted object, and terrible monster Leiber described in those works with the mere word count allotted to this project. A how-to guide for running your fifth edition campaign set in the world of Nehwon would similarly be far beyond the scope of this work.

Instead, like that single chapter in the original *Deities & Demigods*, the reader should treat this work as an introduction to Nehwon and the city of Lankhmar, a sample of monsters and magic to challenge your players, no matter in what world their adventures take place. In time, if interest deems it necessary, Goodman Games may further explore the world and tales of Fafhrd and Mouser in the fifth edition format.

Until then, I hope the following pages set your imaginations aflame and inspire you to journey to the world of Nehwon and its major metropolis, Lankhmar, the City of the Black Toga. If you've never had the pleasure of reading Leiber's stories, consider this to be your invitation to experience some of the greatest sword & sorcery tales ever written. Seek out Leiber's anthologies and get ready to be entertained. I'll be waiting for you at the Silver Eel when you're finished!

— Michael Curtis, 2022

A BIBLIOGRAPHY OF NEHWON SOURCES

Fritz Leiber wrote dozens of short stories, poems, novellas, and novels telling the tales of Fafhrd and the Gray Mouser between the years of 1939 and 1988, a period spanning almost fifty years. Because of the sheer amount of Nehwon fiction published, new readers often have difficulty choosing a story to begin with, while more experienced readers might not find all of Leiber's tales to their liking. Nevertheless, any GM desiring to run a Lankhmar campaign needs to have at least a passing familiarity with the source material. Possessing knowledge of Fritz's stories is invaluable when running or playing RPGs in the world of Nehwon.

The following list covers every piece of Fafhrd and Gray Mouser fiction Leiber penned during his lifetime, plus two others not written by Fritz. Many can be found in the various collections produced by publishing houses such as Ace Books, Gregg Press, White Wolf Publishing, or Dark Horse Books, but a few are more difficult to locate. The stories presented in bold below are, in this author's opinion, the quintessential Fafhrd and Gray Mouser stories and are required reading for any Lankhmar GM or player.

The Jewels in the Forest (1939, as "Two Sought Adventure")

The Bleak Shore (1940)

The Howling Tower (1941)

The Sunken Land (1942)

Thieves' House (1943)

Gray Mouser: 1 (1944)[1]

Gray Mouser: 2 (1944)[1]

Adept's Gambit (1947)[2]

Claws from the Night (1951, as "Dark Vengeance")

The Seven Black Priests (1953)

Induction (1957)

Lean Times in Lankhmar (1959)

When the Sea-King's Away (1960)

Scylla's Daughter (1961)[3]

The Unholy Grail (1962)

Bazaar of the Bizarre (1963)

The Cloud of Hate (1963)

The Lords of Quarmall (1964)[4]

Stardock (1965)

The Swords of Lankhmar (1968)

Their Mistress, the Sea (1968)

The Wrong Branch (1968)

In the Witch's Tent (1968)

The Two Best Thieves in Lankhmar (1968)

The Circle Curse (1970)

The Snow Women (1970)

Ill Met in Lankhmar (1970)

The Price of Pain-Ease (1970)

The Sadness of the Executioner (1973)

Trapped in the Shadowland (1973)

The Bait (1973)

Beauty and the Beasts (1974)

Under the Thumbs of the Gods (1975)

Trapped in the Sea of Stars (1975)

The Frost Monstreme (1976)

Rime Isle (1977)

Sea Magic (1977)

The Mer She (1978)

The Childhood and Youth of the Gray Mouser (1978)[5]

The Curse of the Smalls and the Stars (1983)

Slack Lankhmar Afternoon Featuring Hisvet (1988)[6]

The Mouser Goes Below (1988)[6]

"The Tale of the Grain Ships": A Fragment (1997)

Swords Against the Shadowland (1998)[7]

[1] "Gray Mouser: 1" and "Gray Mouser: 2" are each short poems. They can be found in *Ill Met in Lankhmar* (White Wolf Publishing, 1995).

[2] "Adept's Gambit" was actually the first Fafhrd & Gray Mouser story ever written (1936), but was rejected by *Weird Tales* and didn't see print until 1947.

[3] Began as "The Tale of the Grain Ships" in 1936, but the story became the prototype for "Scylla's Daughter" and later *The Swords of Lankhmar*.

[4] Harry Otto Fischer wrote the first 10k words of "The Lords of Quarmall" in 1936, but it was Leiber who finished the tale and saw it published in 1964.

[5] "The Childhood and Youth of the Gray Mouser" was written by Leiber's long-time friend and co-creator of Fafhrd and the Gray Mouser, Harry Otto Fischer. It was published in *The Dragon* #18.

[6] These two stories were combined into one when published in *The Knight and Knave of Swords* (1988).

[7] *Swords Against the Shadowland* was written by Robin Wayne Bailey and was authorized by Leiber.

PART ONE: NEHWONIAN NASTIES

Fafhrd and the Gray Mouser crossed swords with many fearsome adversaries during their adventures across Nehwon. Most were human, fellow thieves and warriors working to deny the Twain their sought-after loot or sinister sorcerers invoking fell magics against them. Sometimes, however, the two best thieves in Lankhmar (at least, as far as they are concerned) pitted themselves against opponents of a more monstrous nature. This chapter examines some of the creatures both fair and foul that call Nehwon home.

ADDITIONAL MONSTERS IN A LANKHMAR CAMPAIGN

The creatures detailed in this section are just a selection of possible monsters characters might encounter as they explore the world of Nehwon. The Fafhrd and Gray Mouser tales embody the original sword & sorcery genre. As such, some of the pulpier monsters published for the original fantasy roleplaying game fit seamlessly into a campaign set on Nehwon. The following are good additional monsters to include:

aboleth, animated objects, banshee, chuul, cloaker, crawling claw, darkmantle, demilich, demons (all types), devils (all types), dryad, fungi (all types), gargoyle, gibbering mouther, golems (all types), grick, grimlock, hags (all types), homunculus, invisible stalker, kraken, lycanthropes (all types, but especially wererats), merrow, mimic, nagas (all types), ogres, oozes (all types), peryton, purple worm, rakshasa, remorhazes, sahuagin, scarecrow, shambling mound, shield guardian, slaadi (all types), stirge, succubus/incubus, troglodyte, undead (all types), water weird, yeti

Note: Throughout this work a creature name in **bold** is a cue for the GM to refer to that creature's statistics block in the core rules.

A NOTE ON LANGUAGES

The languages of Nehwon don't seamlessly match those presented in the fifth edition. As such, each monster capable of speech is given two entries in its stat block, one of which is in parentheses. The first language item is their known form of speech in the fifth edition rule set. The bracketed entry is the Nehwonian language that they speak or comprehend.

BEHEMOTH

Behemoths are massive beasts that thunder across Nehwon, encountered anywhere from the wooded thickets of the Forest Land to the arid Eastern Deserts to the dense jungle of Klesh. They bear both tusks and tearing teeth, and are protected by a thick, wrinkly hide that has been known to shrug off spears and arrows. Cursed with poor eyesight, a behemoth negotiates its surroundings with its keen hearing and by using its thunderous bellows as a form of echolocation. Despite their massive size and weight of several tons, behemoths move alarmingly fast and are capable of running down both man and beast. Tanned behemoth hide is made into garments and footwear expected to suffer great wear and tear.

BEHEMOTH

Huge beast, unaligned

Armor Class: 15 (natural armor)
Hit Points: 162 (12d12 + 84)
Speed: 40 ft.

STR	DEX	CON	INT	WIS	CHR
25 (+7)	8 (-1)	24 (+7)	3 (-4)	12 (+1)	6 (-2)

Skills: Perception +4
Senses: blindsight 120 ft., passive Perception 14
Languages: —
Challenge: 7 (2,900 XP)

Echolocation: The behemoth can't use its blindsight while deafened.

Keen Hearing: The behemoth has advantage on Wisdom (Perception) checks that rely on hearing.

Trampling Charge: If the behemoth moves at least 20 feet straight toward a creature and then hits it with its tusks on the same turn, the target must succeed on a DC 18 Strength saving throw or be knocked prone. If the target is prone, the behemoth can make one stomp attack against it as a bonus action.

OF BEHEMOTHS AND LEVIATHANS

The creatures known as behemoths and leviathans are mentioned several times in the course of the Fafhrd and the Gray Mouser stories, but neither are encountered directly by the duo. A careful reading of the stories suggests that these mysterious creatures may in fact be nothing more than elephants and whales, respectively. While this is a valid reading of the source material, it leaves something to be desired in the scope of a fantasy roleplaying game. Therefore, the author has provided alternate descriptions and stats for monstrous creatures. We leave it to the individual Game Masters to decide what behemoths and leviathans actually are in their campaigns.

ACTIONS

Bite: *Melee Weapon Attack:* +10 to hit, reach 5 ft., one target. *Hit:* 24 (5d6 + 7) piercing damage.

Tusks: *Melee Weapon Attack:* +10 to hit, reach 10 ft., one target. *Hit:* 25 (4d8 + 7) piercing damage.

Stomp: *Melee Weapon Attack:* +10 to hit, reach 5 ft., one prone target. *Hit:* 29 (4d10 + 7) bludgeoning damage.

BELOVED OF TYAA

The Beloved of Tyaa are black birds sized slightly larger than crows and display uncanny intelligence for an avian species. They are said to have been blessed by the goddess Winged Tyaa, raised up above all other birds to serve her most devoted priestesses and their servants, the Falconers of Tyaa. When serving a priestess or other adherent of Winged Tyaa, their claws are usually smeared with poison, making them dangerous opponents.

BELOVED OF TYAA

Tiny beast, unaligned

Armor Class: 12

Hit Points: 2 (1d4)

Speed: 10 ft., fly 50 ft.

STR	DEX	CON	INT	WIS	CHR
2 (-4)	14 (+2)	10 (+0)	8 (-1)	12 (+1)	6 (-2)

Skills: Perception +3, Sleight of Hand +4

Senses: passive Perception 13

Languages: understands Common but can't speak (understands Low Lankhmarese but can't speak)

Challenge: 1/8 (25 XP)

Mimicry: The Beloved of Tyaa can mimic simple sounds it has heard, such as a person whispering, a baby crying, or an animal chittering. A creature that hears the sounds can tell they are imitations with a successful DC 10 Wisdom (Insight) check.

ACTIONS

Beak: *Melee Weapon Attack:* +4 to hit, reach 5 ft., one target. *Hit:* 1 piercing damage.

Claws: *Melee Weapon Attack:* +4 to hit, reach 5 ft., one target. *Hit:* 1 slashing damage, and the target must make a DC 10 Constitution saving throw, taking 5 (2d4) poison damage on a failed save, or half as much damage on a successful one.

BLEAK SHORE EXECUTIONER

These peculiar creatures are believed to exist solely on a lonely strand on the far side of the Outer Sea, dwelling on a desolate beach known as the Bleak Shore. Resembling a terrible mixture of reptile, bird, and crustacean, Bleak

Shore executioners walk erect on lizard-like clawed feet and stand taller than a man. Their bodies are covered by a carapace adorned with jagged spikes and their reptilian heads are protected by bone plates and crests resembling armored helms. Their arms each end in a yard-long claw capable of eviscerating their opponents.

BLEAK SHORE EXECUTIONER

Medium monstrosity, lawful evil

Armor Class: 16 (natural armor)

Hit Points: 52 (8d8 + 16)

Speed: 30 ft.

STR	DEX	CON	INT	WIS	CHR
16 (+3)	16 (+3)	15 (+2)	6 (-2)	10 (+0)	6 (-2)

Damage Resistances: necrotic

Damage Immunities: poison

Condition Immunities: charmed, exhaustion, poisoned

Senses: darkvision 60 ft., passive Perception 10

Languages: —

Challenge: 2 (450 XP)

Life Connection: The Bleak Shore executioner's life force is connected to a strange, bald, almost embryonic creature that dwells inside a large egg on the Bleak Shore. Slaying this weird creature instantly kills the Bleak Shore executioner.

ACTIONS

Multiattack: The Bleak Shore executioner attacks twice with its claws.

Claws: *Melee Weapon Attack:* +5 to hit, reach 5 ft., one target. *Hit:* 10 (2d6 + 3) slashing damage.

REACTIONS

Parry: The Bleak Shore executioner adds 3 to its AC against one melee attack that would hit it. To do so, the Bleak Shore executioner must see the attacker and have use of at least one of its claws.

DRAGON OF NEHWON (SEA SERPENT)

Dragons in Nehwon are not the winged, fire-breathing variety common to other world bubbles, but are instead a species of great aquatic or amphibious scaly beasts found in its waters. Dragons of Nehwon range in appearance: some possess two heads; others have stubby, feet-like flippers that allow them to move on land; others bear large, fantastic crests atop their heads for attracting mates. In addition to varying in appearance, Nehwonian dragons also display an array of temperaments. Some are violent, attacking anything they encounter, while others are playful and sport with ships at sea. When designing a Nehwonian dragon, the GM should use the stats provided as a baseline and roll on the table below to determine any additional physical characteristics it possesses. A second table is provided to adjudicate the dragon's initial attitude towards the party.

Note: Traits and attacks marked with an asterisk may not apply to all dragons of Nehwon. See the Dragon Appearance table below.

DRAGON OF NEHWON

Huge dragon, unaligned

Armor Class: 17 (natural armor)

Hit Points: 184 (16d12 + 80)

Speed: 0 ft., swim 40 ft.

STR	DEX	CON	INT	WIS	CHR
22 (+6)	14 (+2)	20 (+5)	7 (-2)	11 (+0)	8 (-1)

Skills: Athletics +9, Perception +3

Senses: darkvision 60 ft., passive Perception 13

Languages: —

Challenge: 7 (2,900 XP) (Base, see below)

Hold Breath: The dragon of Nehwon can hold its breath for 1 hour.

ACTIONS

*Multiattack: The dragon of Nehwon makes multiple attacks, one of which is a bite. See the Dragon Appearance table below for more information.

Bite: *Melee Weapon Attack:* +9 to hit, reach 10 ft., one target. *Hit:* 20 (4d6 + 6) piercing damage.

*Gore: *Melee Weapon Attack:* +6 to hit, reach 10 ft., one target. *Hit:* 16 (3d6 + 6) piercing damage.

*Poison Stinger: *Melee Weapon Attack:* +9 to hit, reach 15 ft., one target. *Hit:* 16 (3d6 + 6) piercing damage, and the target must make a DC 15 Constitution saving throw, taking 27 (6d8) poison damage on a failed save, or half as much damage on a successful one.

*Tail Slap: *Melee Weapon Attack:* +9 to hit, reach 15 ft., one target. *Hit:* 15 (2d8 + 6) bludgeoning damage.

CUSTOMIZED DRAGONS OF NEHWON

The dragons of Nehwon come in so many different varieties that it would require an entire chapter to include stat blocks detailing every possible combination. Instead, the GM can decide whether the dragon is a "stock dragon" as described in the stat block above or has additional traits and actions. If the GM opts for the second choice, they can roll 1d4 times on the table below and apply the appropriate features to the base dragon. Due to the possible permutations the table provides, the GM may have to recalculate the creature's challenge rating using the methods described in chapter 9 of the *Dungeon Master's Guide*.

Dragon Appearance (Roll 1d4 times)

d12	Dragon has…
1	Two heads (can use Multiattack to make two bite attacks)
2	Three heads (can use Multiattack to make three bite attacks)
3	Flippers capable of walking on dry land (gains a walking speed of 20 feet)
4	Horns (can use a bonus action to make a gore attack)
5	Crest on its head (+1 bonus to AC)
6	Crest along its spine (+1 bonus to AC)
7	Two tails (can use Multiattack to attack with its bite and a tail slap)
8	Three eyes on each head (gains the Keen Sight trait)
9	Poisonous stinger on tail (can use a bonus action to make a poison stinger attack)
10	Great size (increase size to Gargantuan and hit points become 248 [16d20 + 80])
11	Stalwart constitution (has advantage on Constitution saving throws)
12	Uncanny agility (+2 bonus to AC and has advantage on Dexterity saving throws)

INITIAL ATTITUDE

Dragons of Nehwon possess many personalities. Some are highly aggressive, wantonly attacking any creature or ship that strays into their territories. Others have been known to cavort with swimmers or follow ships hoping for handouts. Still others just want to be left alone. When the party encounters a dragon of Nehwon in the wild, the GM can use the following table to determine the creature's initial attitude towards the group and how it might react to their presence.

Dragon Attitude (Roll once when dragon is first encountered)

d12	Dragon attitude is…
1-3	Hostile and attacks immediately!
4-6	Hostile and has 50% chance of attacking.
7-8	Indifferent and wishes to be left alone.
9-10	Indifferent, but has a 50% chance of sporting with the characters. Otherwise ignores them.
11-12	Friendly and sports with the characters unless provoked.

FISH-OF-THE-AIR

Fish-of-the-air are great, invisible, and furred flying fish bearing a keen resemblance to ocean-going manta rays. A mass of 10 small tentacles rings their gaping mouths, and they use these to both feed on small birds, lichen, and mosses, and to grip the rocky precipices upon which they lair. Fish-of-the-air are used by the Invisibles of Stardock as winged mounts and each beast can accommodate up to four Medium riders. Usually placid beasts, fish-of-the-air defend themselves by buffeting foes with their large wings.

FISH-OF-THE-AIR

Large beast, unaligned

Armor Class: 13 (natural armor)

Hit Points: 32 (5d10 + 5)

Speed: 10 ft., fly 40 ft.

STR	DEX	CON	INT	WIS	CHR
16 (+3)	14 (+2)	12 (+1)	6 (-2)	10 (+0)	6 (-2)

Saving Throws: Con +3

Damage Resistances: cold

Senses: blindsight 30 ft., passive Perception 10

Languages: —

Challenge: 1/4 (50 XP)

Invisibility: The fish-of-the-air is invisible.

ACTIONS

Wing Attack: The fish-of-the-air beats its wings. Each creature within 10 feet of the fish-of-the-air must succeed on a DC 12 Dexterity saving throw or take 5 (2d4) bludgeoning damage and be knocked prone. The fish-of-the-air can then fly up to half its flying speed.

GHOST HOUND

Ghost hounds are the spiritual echoes of once-faithful dogs that died from hunger or due to their owner's neglect. They exist outside the physical world of Nehwon, lurking in the spiritual hinterlands just beyond the borders of this dimension and the Shadowland. Ghost hounds are ethereal and unable to harm creatures on the Material Plane, but are terrors in the Ethereal netherworld. Ghost hounds are invisible to the naked eye and can only sometimes be perceived by their faint howls heard on the wind.

Ghost hounds typically exist until the target of their hatred, usually the person or persons responsible for their death, is slain by the undead dogs, its soul torn apart in the afterlife. The ghost hound fades away once its vengeance is achieved.

GHOST HOUND

Small undead, unaligned

Armor Class: 12

Hit Points: 4 (1d6 + 1)

Speed: 40 ft.

STR	DEX	CON	INT	WIS	CHR
10 (+0)	14 (+2)	12 (+1)	3 (-4)	12 (+1)	7 (-2)

Skills: Perception +3

Damage Resistances: bludgeoning, piercing, and slashing that is nonmagical

Damage Immunities: cold, necrotic, poison

Condition Immunities: charmed, exhaustion, frightened, petrified, poisoned, restrained

Senses: passive Perception 13

Languages: —

Challenge: 1/4 (50 XP)

Ethereal: The ghost hound exists solely on the Ethereal Plane and is only sensed on the Material Plane as a wailing howl. It is immune to all attacks and spells originating on the Material Plane unless they specifically affect creatures on the Ethereal Plane.

Keen Hearing and Smell: The ghost hound has advantage on Wisdom (Perception) checks that rely on hearing or smell.

Undead Nature: The ghost hound doesn't require air, food, drink, or sleep.

ACTIONS

Bite: *Melee Weapon Attack:* +4 to hit, reach 5 ft., one target. *Hit:* 4 (1d4 + 2) piercing damage, and the target is grappled (escape DC 12) by the ghost hound's locked jaws. While its jaws are locked, the ghost hound does not attack. Until the grapple ends, the target automatically suffers 4 (1d4 + 2) piercing damage at the start of each of its turns, as the ghost hound worries its opponent. Up to two ghost hounds can worry a Small creature, three can worry a Medium target, and five hounds can worry a Large or larger target at one time.

GODS OF LANKHMAR

Lankhmar City was founded near a strange and antediluvian temple close to the River Hlal. It is said in hushed circles that the city's founders agreed to an eldritch compact with the denizens of that temple, making an alliance that allowed the city to prosper and become the metropolis it is today. Despite the shuttered doors of the temple and its overall appearance of neglect, the fane remains occupied by those feared entities known as the Gods of Lankhmar (not to be confused with the Gods *in* Lankhmar).

The Gods of Lankhmar seldom emerge from their temple, coming forth only to defend the city and then chastise its residents for allowing matters to reach a point where they had to intervene, or to neutralize a threat to their own prominence in ecclesiastical matters within the city. The Gods of Lankhmar appear as humanoid mummies clad in brown, desiccated flesh and garbed in the iconic black togas of the city. Each bears a black rod that withers the living when it strikes them.

It is unknown how many Gods of Lankhmar dwell in their black temple. Rumors abound that 13 of these powerful entities exist in crypts under the city, but this is pure speculation. When the Gods of Lankhmar emerged during the Rat War, most Lankhmarts were too busy fleeing to count their numbers, and if Fafhrd took the time to note how many came forth, the great barbarian has been silent on the matter.

GOD OF LANKHMAR

A God of Lankhmar has identical stats as a **mummy lord** with the following additional attack, which may be used as part of its Multiattack action:

Black Staff (Recharge 4-6): *Melee Weapon Attack:* +9 to hit, reach 5 ft., one target. *Hit:* 8 (1d8 + 4) bludgeoning damage plus 22 (4d10) necrotic damage, and the target must succeed on a DC 15 Constitution saving throw or have disadvantage for 1 hour on any ability check or saving throw that uses Strength or Constitution. If the God of Lankhmar is ever permanently destroyed, its black staff crumbles into dust.

ICE GNOME

Ice gnomes are brutish humanoids standing 4 feet tall. Their bodies are stout, broad, and thick-limbed, and their faces are of ugly countenance. Ice gnomes are largely bald and possess wide, thick-lipped mouths that seem to spread from ear to ear. They dwell in the Cold Waste, living in extended clans found from the shores of the Frozen Sea to the Mountains of the Giants. Ice gnomes seldom stray from their small enclaves, but during high summer they range across the Cold Waste in lemming-like hordes, scavenging and raiding to collect the resources they need to survive the long northern winters. Ice gnomes vary in temperament; some trade readily with southern humans while others are devoted enemies to the northern barbarians. Some are said to pay homage to the Invisibles of Stardock.

Ice gnomes are incredibly strong for their small size and are adept wrestlers. They dress in leather or hide armor when going on raids or defending their holdings, wielding iron weapons they acquire through trade or plunder. Ice gnomes do not practice wizardry, but legend maintains that they can summon a chilling cold when assembled in large numbers.

ICE GNOME

Small humanoid (ice gnome), lawful neutral

Armor Class: 14 (hide armor)

Hit Points: 26 (4d6 + 12)

Speed: 20 ft.

STR	DEX	CON	INT	WIS	CHR
16 (+3)	14 (+2)	16 (+3)	11 (+0)	9 (-1)	7 (-2)

Skills: Athletics +5, Perception +1, Survival +1

Damage Immunities: cold

Senses: passive Perception 11

Languages: Common, Gnomish, plus any one language (Low Lankhmarese, the Cold Tongue, plus any one language)

Challenge: 1/4 (50 XP)

Summon Cold: A group of six or more ice gnomes can each use their action to create a chilling cold at a range of 120 feet. The cold snap affects a 15-foot-radius sphere. Each creature in the sphere when it appears or that ends its turn there must make a DC 10 Constitution saving throw or take 9 (2d8) cold damage. The ground within the sphere is icy and becomes difficult terrain. The cold lasts for either 1 minute or

immediately dissipates if the number of ice gnomes responsible for creating it is reduced to 5 or fewer. No group of ice gnomes can create this effect more than 3 times per day.

ACTIONS

War Pick: *Melee Weapon Attack:* +5 to hit, reach 5 ft., one target. *Hit:* 7 (1d8 + 3) piercing damage.

Javelin: *Melee or Ranged Weapon Attack:* +5 to hit, reach 5 ft. or range 30/120 ft., one target. *Hit:* 6 (1d6 + 3) piercing damage.

INVISIBLES OF STARDOCK

The Invisibles of Stardock are an ancient but dying race. Their bodies are completely transparent, invisible to the naked eye, although objects carried and garments worn by them are visible. For this reason, most Invisibles go naked aside from their weapons. Females of the race are known to utilize makeup and body paint when wishing to be glimpsed by "lower order" races. Some Invisibles are arcane spellcasters, primarily wizards. These mystically-inclined Invisibles tend to be of the race's upper nobility and are rarely encountered away from Stardock.

INVISIBLE OF STARDOCK

Medium humanoid (Invisible of Stardock), neutral evil

Armor Class: 12

Hit Points: 22 (3d8 + 9)

Speed: 30 ft.

STR	DEX	CON	INT	WIS	CHR
13 (+1)	15 (+2)	16 (+3)	14 (+2)	11 (+0)	11 (+0)

Skills: Animal Handling +2, Perception +2, Survival +2

Damage Immunities: cold

Senses: truesight 60 ft., passive Perception 12

Languages: Common, Primordial, plus any one language (Low Lankhmarese, High Lankhmarese, the Invisible

Speak, plus any one language)

Challenge: 1/8 (25 XP)

Invisibility: The Invisible of Stardock is invisible.

ACTIONS

Spear: *Melee or Ranged Weapon Attack:* +3 to hit, reach 5 ft. or 20/60 ft., one target. *Hit:* 4 (1d6 + 1) piercing damage, or 5 (1d8 + 1) piercing damage if used with two hands to make a melee attack.

Sling: *Ranged Weapon Attack:* +4 to hit, range 30/120 ft., one target. *Hit:* 4 (1d4 + 2) bludgeoning damage.

INVISIBLE OF STARDOCK DUELIST

Medium humanoid (Invisible of Stardock), neutral evil

Armor Class: 13

Hit Points: 45 (6d8 + 18)

Speed: 30 ft.

STR	DEX	CON	INT	WIS	CHR
15 (+2)	16 (+3)	16 (+3)	12 (+1)	13 (+1)	11 (+0)

Skills: Perception +3, Survival +3

Damage Immunities: cold

Senses: truesight 60 ft., passive Perception 13

Languages: Common, Primordial, plus any one language (Low Lankhmarese, High Lankhmarese, the Invisible Speak, plus any one language)

Challenge: 1/2 (100 XP)

Invisibility: The Invisible of Stardock duelist is invisible.

ACTIONS

Multiattack: The Invisible of Stardock duelist makes one attack with its longsword and one attack with its dagger.

Longsword: *Melee Weapon Attack:* +4 to hit, reach 5 ft., one target. *Hit:* 6 (1d8 + 2) slashing damage, or 7 (1d10 + 2) slashing damage if used with two hands.

Dagger: *Melee or Ranged Weapon Attack:* +5 to hit, reach 5 ft. or 20/60 ft., one target. *Hit:* 5 (1d4 + 3) piercing damage.

REACTIONS

Parry: The Invisible of Stardock duelist adds 2 to its AC against one melee attack that would hit it. To do so, the Invisible of Stardock duelist must see the attack and be wielding a melee weapon.

INVISIBLE OF STARDOCK NOBLE WIZARD

Medium humanoid (Invisible of Stardock), neutral evil

Armor Class: 12 (15 with *mage armor*)

Hit Points: 39 (6d8 + 12)

Speed: 30 ft.

STR	DEX	CON	INT	WIS	CHR
11 (+0)	15 (+2)	15 (+2)	16 (+3)	12 (+1)	14 (+2)

Skills: Animal Handling +3, Arcana +5, History +5, Survival +3

Damage Immunities: cold

Senses: truesight 60 ft., passive Perception 11

Languages: Common, Primordial, plus any two languages (Low Lankhmarese, High Lankhmarese, the Invisible Speak, plus any two languages)

Challenge: 2 (450 XP)

Invisibility: The Invisible of Stardock noble wizard is invisible.

Spellcasting: The Invisible of Stardock noble wizard is a 6th-level spellcaster. Its spellcasting ability is Intelligence (spell save DC 13, +5 to hit with spell attacks). The Invisible of Stardock noble wizard has the following wizard spells prepared:

- Cantrips (at will): *chill touch, dancing lights, minor illusion, ray of frost*
- 1st level (4 slots): *feather fall, mage armor, shield, witch bolt*
- 2nd level (3 slots): *hold person, ray of enfeeblement, see invisibility*
- 3rd level (3 slots): *fly, lightning bolt*

ACTIONS

Scimitar: *Melee Weapon Attack:* +4 to hit, reach 5 ft., one target. *Hit:* 5 (1d6 + 2) slashing damage.

KLESHITE GHOUL

Not to be confused with the transparent-skinned denizens of the northern lands, Kleshite ghouls dwell in the dense tropical jungle in the south. These creatures range from dark brown to light tan in coloration and resemble gaunt humanoids with dirt-matted hair and dense, abrased skin. Kleshite ghouls have shovel-like hands which they use to both burrow through the earth at a fast rate and to attack and pin their prey. They dwell predominantly around graveyards and burial grounds, although they only feast on carrion and corpses when fresher, livelier food is wanting. Kleshite ghouls prefer to attack from ambush, bursting from the earth to grab their prey, which they drag back to their burrows or consume on the spot. Although it is unknown if Kleshite ghouls and Nehwon ghouls are related, like Nehwon ghouls, Kleshite ghouls are not undead creatures and are unaffected by effects baneful specifically to undead.

KLESHITE GHOUL

Medium monstrosity, neutral evil

Armor Class: 12 (natural armor)

Hit Points: 22 (4d8 + 4)

Speed: 30 ft., burrow 20 ft.

STR	DEX	CON	INT	WIS	CHR
14 (+2)	12 (+1)	12 (+1)	8 (-1)	12 (+1)	8 (-1)

Skills: Athletics +4, Perception +3

Senses: tremorsense 60 ft., passive Perception 13

Languages: Common (Kleshic)

Challenge: 1/4 (50 XP)

Keen Smell: The Kleshite ghoul has advantage on Wisdom (Perception) checks that rely on smell.

Pin: If the Kleshite ghoul knocks an opponent prone, it can make an opposed Strength (Athletics) check vs. the target's Strength (Athletics) or Dexterity (Acrobatics) check as a bonus action. If the Kleshite ghoul wins the check, it pins the creature beneath it and the target is grappled (escape DC 14). Until this grapple ends the target is restrained.

ACTIONS

Slam: *Melee Weapon Attack:* +4 to hit, reach 5 ft., one target. *Hit:* 6 (1d8 + 2) bludgeoning damage, and the target must succeed on a DC 12 Strength saving throw or be knocked prone.

Bite: *Melee Weapon Attack:* +4 to hit, reach 5 ft., one target. *Hit:* 2 (1d4 + 2) piercing damage.

LEVIATHAN

Leviathans are monstrous sea creatures measuring up to 100 feet in length. They are horrible brutes with dark-colored flesh partially covered by bony plates around the head and back, rows of razor-sharp teeth, and a general desire to be left alone. Leviathans have few natural predators, but daring seagoing civilizations regularly hunt smaller specimens for their blubber that can be rendered to make flammable, clean-burning oil.

LEVIATHAN

Gargantuan beast, unaligned

Armor Class: 13 (natural armor)

Hit Points: 250 (20d20 + 40)

Speed: 0 ft., swim 60 ft.

STR	DEX	CON	INT	WIS	CHR
22 (+6)	10 (+0)	15 (+2)	3 (-4)	12 (+1)	6 (-2)

Skills: Perception +4

Damage Resistances: cold; bludgeoning from nonmagical attacks

Senses: blindsight 120 ft., passive Perception 14

Languages: —

Challenge: 7 (2,900 XP)

Echolocation: The leviathan can't use its blindsight while deafened.

Hold Breath: The leviathan can hold its breath for 1 hour.

Keen Hearing: The leviathan has advantage on Wisdom (Perception) checks that rely on hearing.

Siege Monster: The leviathan deals double damage to objects and structures.

ACTIONS

Bite: *Melee Weapon Attack:* +9 to hit, reach 5 ft., one target. *Hit:* 17 (2d10 + 6) piercing damage. If the target is a Large or smaller creature, it must succeed on a DC 11 Dexterity saving throw or be swallowed by the leviathan. A swallowed creature is blinded and restrained, it has total cover against attacks and other effects outside the leviathan, and takes 21 (6d6) acid damage at the start of each of the leviathan's turns.

If the leviathan takes 30 damage or more on a single turn from the creature inside it, the leviathan must succeed on a DC 15 Constitution saving throw at the end of that turn or regurgitate all swallowed creatures, which fall prone in a space within 10 feet of the leviathan. If the leviathan dies, a swallowed creature is no longer restrained by it and can escape from the corpse by using 15 feet of movement, exiting prone.

Ram: *Melee Weapon Attack:* +9 to hit, reach 10 ft., one target. *Hit:* 20 (4d6 + 6) bludgeoning damage.

NEHWON GHOULS

Nehwon ghouls appear as skeletons, their flesh, internal organs, and even blood being transparent. This nature hints at some long-ago shared heritage with the Invisibles of Stardock. Nehwon ghouls' skeletal appearance impedes ranged attacks directed at them. Nehwon ghouls are cannibals and consider it their sacred duty to transform the opaque flesh of other creatures into crystal clear purity by digesting it. They are ferocious fighters and greatly feared by all in Nehwon.

Nehwon ghouls are usually encountered in the lands around the Sea of Monsters, upon which the fabled and feared City of Ghouls stands. They range out from this region to battle and hunt the Mingols of the Steppes and have been known to launch raids as far as the coast of the Inner Sea. Those not killed in battle are enslaved and brought back to the City of Ghouls to feed its inhabitants.

NEHWON GHOUL

Medium humanoid (Nehwon ghoul), neutral evil

Armor Class: 13 (shield)

Hit Points: 26 (4d8 + 8)

Speed: 30 ft.

STR	DEX	CON	INT	WIS	CHR
15 (+2)	12 (+1)	14 (+2)	11 (+0)	10 (+0)	8 (-1)

Skills: Intimidation +1, Survival +2

Senses: darkvision 60 ft., passive Perception 10

Languages: Common (Low Lankhmarese, Old Ghoulish)

Challenge: 1 (200 XP)

Difficult to Target: The Nehwon ghoul has a +2 AC modifier against ranged attacks due to its transparent body.

Frightful Reputation: Each creature attempting to attack the Nehwon ghoul must succeed on a DC 10 Wisdom saving throw or be frightened for 1 minute. A creature can repeat the saving throw at the end of each of its turns, ending the effect on itself on a success. If a creature's saving throw is successful or the effect ends for it, the creature is

immune to Frightful Reputation from any Nehwon ghoul for 24 hours.

ACTIONS

Longsword: *Melee Weapon Attack:* +4 to hit, reach 5 ft., one target. *Hit:* 6 (1d8 + 2) slashing damage, or 7 (1d10 + 2) slashing damage if used with two hands.

Shortbow: *Ranged Weapon Attack:* +3 to hit, range 80/320 ft., one target. *Hit:* 4 (1d6 + 1) piercing damage.

NEHWON GHOUL RAID CAPTAIN

Medium humanoid (Nehwon ghoul), neutral evil

Armor Class: 14 (shield)

Hit Points: 52 (8d8 + 16)

Speed: 30 ft.

STR	DEX	CON	INT	WIS	CHR
16 (+3)	14 (+2)	15 (+2)	11 (+0)	10 (+0)	12 (+1)

Skills: Intimidation +3, Survival +2

Senses: darkvision 60 ft., passive Perception 10

Languages: Common (Low Lankhmarese, Old Ghoulish)

Challenge: 2 (450 XP)

Difficult to Target: The Nehwon ghoul raid captain has a +2 AC modifier against ranged attacks due to its transparent body.

Frightful Reputation: Each creature attempting to attack the Nehwon ghoul raid captain must succeed on a DC 10 Wisdom saving throw or be frightened for 1 minute. A creature can repeat the saving throw at the end of each of its turns, ending the effect on itself on a success. If a creature's saving throw is successful or the effect ends for it, the creature is immune to Frightful Reputation from any Nehwon ghoul for 24 hours.

ACTIONS

Multiattack: The Nehwon ghoul raid captain attacks twice with its greataxe.

Greataxe: *Melee Weapon Attack:* +5 to hit, reach 5 ft., one target. *Hit:* 9 (1d12 + 3) slashing damage.

Shortbow: *Ranged Weapon Attack:* +4 to hit, range 80/320 ft., one target. *Hit:* 5 (1d6 + 2) piercing damage.

RATS OF LANKHMAR BELOW

The rats of Lankhmar Below are a unique species of vermin possessing human-level intelligence due to generations of interbreeding with humankind. Their existence was unknown for centuries save only to certain debase noble families and the priest of Ilthmar's Rat God, but after a failed coup against Lankhmar, the denizens of the city are now aware of the danger that scurries beneath their feet. The rats of Lankhmar Below are cunning opponents who, knowing they're outsized by their human foes, employ a variety of tactics against them. Poison, arson, and trap-setting are used whenever possible and the rats only engage people in direct combat when their numbers negate humankind's size advantage. In addition to their own kind, the rats of Lankhmar Below also use the unintelligent species of vermin common in the city and can corral and drive **swarms of rats** against their hated foes in Lankhmar Above. Unlike normal rats, the rats of Lankhmar Below seldom carry disease themselves, but readily use normal rats as plague carriers when tactics deem necessary.

Two sets of stats are provided for the rats of Lankhmar Below. The first is for when the rats are encountered in their normal animal size, typically on excursions to Lankhmar Above. The second stats are used when either the rats have grown to human-size or when humans have shrunk to rat-size and both species are of comparative size and mass.

RAT OF LANKHMAR BELOW (RAT-SIZED)

Tiny humanoid (rat of Lankhmar Below), lawful evil

Armor Class: 12 (leather armor)

Hit Points: 3 (1d4 + 1)

Speed: 20 ft.

STR	DEX	CON	INT	WIS	CHR
4 (-3)	12 (+1)	12 (+1)	10 (+0)	10 (+0)	6 (-2)

Skills: Stealth +3

Senses: darkvision 30 ft., passive Perception 10

Languages: Common (Low Lankhmarese, High Lankhmarese)

Challenge: 1/8 (25 XP)

Keen Smell: The rat of Lankhmar Below has advantage on Wisdom (Perception) checks that rely on smell.

ACTIONS

Bite: *Melee Weapon Attack:* +1 to hit, reach 5 ft., one target. *Hit:* 1 piercing damage.

Tiny Light Crossbow: *Ranged Weapon Attack:* +3 to hit, range 20/80 ft., one target. *Hit:* 1 piercing damage plus 4 (1d8) poison damage.

RAT OF LANKHMAR BELOW (MAN-SIZED)

Medium humanoid (rat of Lankhmar Below), lawful evil

Armor Class: 13 (leather armor)

Hit Points: 11 (2d8 + 2)

Speed: 30 ft.

STR	DEX	CON	INT	WIS	CHR
12 (+1)	15 (+2)	12 (+1)	10 (+0)	10 (+0)	6 (-2)

Skills: Perception +2, Stealth +4

Senses: darkvision 60 ft., passive Perception 12

Languages: Common (Low Lankhmarese, High Lankhmarese)

Challenge: 1/2 (100 XP)

Keen Smell: The rat of Lankhmar Below has advantage on Wisdom (Perception) checks that rely on smell.

ACTIONS

Multiattack: The rat of Lankhmar Below makes two attacks, only one of which can be a bite.

Bite: *Melee Weapon Attack:* +4 to hit, reach 5 ft., one target.

Hit: 4 (1d4 + 2) piercing damage.

Glaive: *Melee Weapon Attack:* +3 to hit, reach 10 ft., one target. *Hit:* 6 (1d10 + 1) slashing damage.

Shortsword: *Melee Weapon Attack:* +4 to hit, reach 5 ft., one target. *Hit:* 5 (1d6 + 2) piercing damage.

Simorgyans

Simorgyans are an ancient race who once ruled an island kingdom located in the Outer Ocean. They were potent wizards with mastery over wind, wave, and the creatures of the deep. Their kingdom sank long ago, and Simorgya was lost beneath the waves. The race was not drowned, however, and many used their sorcery to acclimate themselves to their undersea existence. The Simorgyans are now an aquatic race, but capable of returning to dry land when their schemes require them to, albeit with diminished strength.

In their normal form, Simorgyans are handsome humanoids with silvery scaled skin, hawk-like facial features, and supple fingers terminating in thin claws. They are adept at changing their forms, however, and can disguise themselves as comely, pale humans with silvery-blonde hair and black-rimmed, green eyes when they wish to move about dry land civilizations unnoticed. Simorgyans can also transform themselves into both a hunter shark form and a terrible, humanoid-fish hybrid.

SIMORGYAN

Medium humanoid (Simorgyan, shapechanger), lawful evil

Armor Class: 12 in humanoid form, 13 (natural armor) in hunter shark or hybrid form

Hit Points: 11 (2d8 + 2)

Speed: 30 ft., swim 40 ft.

STR	DEX	CON	INT	WIS	CHR
12 (+1)	15 (+2)	12 (+1)	10 (+0)	10 (+0)	6 (-2)

Skills: Perception +2, Stealth +4

Senses: darkvision 60 ft., passive Perception 12

Languages: Aquan, Common (Simorgyan, Low Lankhmarese)

Challenge: 1/2 (100 XP)

Shapechanger: The Simorgyan can use its action to polymorph into a fish-human hybrid or into a Large **hunter shark**, or back into its true form, which is humanoid. Its statistics, other than its size and AC, are the same in each form. Any equipment it is wearing or carrying isn't transformed. It reverts to its true form if it dies.

Amphibious: The Simorgyan can breathe air and water.

Illusory Appearance: The Simorgyan covers itself and anything it is wearing or carrying with a magical illusion that makes it look like a beautiful humanoid of its general shape and size. The illusion ends if the Simorgyan takes a bonus action to end it or if it dies.

The changes wrought by this effect fail to hold up to physical inspection. For example, someone touching the disguised Simorgyan's bare skin would feel delicate scales instead of soft flesh. Otherwise, a creature must take an action to visually inspect the illusion and succeed on a DC 15 Intelligence (Investigation) check to discern the Simorgyan is disguised.

Incorporeal Form: The Simorgyan can use an action to become incorporeal when in humanoid form and on dry land. All objects carried by the Simorgyan also become incorporeal along with it. The Simorgyan remains incorporeal for 1 minute, or until it uses an action to return to physical form or change out of its humanoid form. The incorporeal state also ends if the Simorgyan comes into contact with salt water or is reduced to 0 hit points.

While in this incorporeal state, it gains the following traits:

- **Damage Resistances:** acid, cold, fire, lightning, poison, thunder; bludgeoning, piercing, and slashing from nonmagical attacks
- **Incorporeal Movement:** The Simorgyan can move through other creatures and objects as if they were difficult terrain. It takes 5 (1d10) force damage if it ends its turn inside an object.
- **Sickening Touch:** The Simorgyan can use the Sickening Touch action.

Sea Tied: The Simorgyan has disadvantage on attack rolls, ability checks, and physical saving throws when in humanoid form and on dry land. If the Simorgyan is on a ship or otherwise surrounded by but not immersed in water then it does not suffer from this effect.

ACTIONS

Multiattack (Humanoid or Hybrid Form Only): The Simorgyan makes two attacks, only one of which can be a bite.

Bite (Hunter Shark or Hybrid Form Only): *Melee Weapon Attack:* +3 to hit, reach 5 ft., one target. *Hit:* 10 (2d8 + 1) piercing damage.

Shortsword (Humanoid or Hybrid Form Only): *Melee Weapon Attack:* +4 to hit, reach 5 ft., one target. *Hit:* 5 (1d6 + 2) piercing damage.

Sickening Touch (Recharge 5-6) (Incorporeal Form Only): *Melee Weapon Attack:* +4 to hit, reach 5 ft., one creature. *Hit:* 9 (2d8) poison damage, and the target must succeed on a DC 11 Constitution saving throw or become poisoned for 1 hour.

SIMORGYAN NOBLE

Medium humanoid (Simorgyan, shapechanger), lawful evil

Armor Class: 16 (scale mail) in humanoid form, 13 (natural armor) in hunter shark or hybrid form

Hit Points: 44 (8d8 + 8)

Speed: 30 ft., swim 40 ft.

STR	DEX	CON	INT	WIS	CHR
12 (+1)	15 (+2)	12 (+1)	14 (+2)	11 (+0)	16 (+3)

Skills: Arcana +4, Deception +5, Perception +2, Stealth +4

Senses: darkvision 60 ft., passive Perception 12

Languages: Aquan, Common (Simorgyan, Low Lankhmarese, High Lankhmarese)

Challenge: 1 (200 XP)

Shapechanger: The Simorgyan noble can use its action to polymorph into a fish-human hybrid or into a Large **hunter shark**, or back into its true form, which is humanoid. Its statistics, other than its size and AC, are the same in each form. Any equipment it is wearing or carrying isn't transformed. It reverts to its true form if it dies.

Amphibious: The Simorgyan noble can breathe air and water.

Illusory Appearance: The Simorgyan noble covers itself and anything it is wearing or carrying with a magical illusion that makes it look like a beautiful humanoid of its general shape and size. The illusion ends if the Simorgyan noble takes a bonus action to end it or if it dies.

The changes wrought by this effect fail to hold up to physical inspection. For example, someone touching the disguised Simorgyan noble's bare skin would feel delicate scales instead of soft flesh. Otherwise, a creature must take an action to visually inspect the illusion and succeed on a DC 15 Intelligence (Investigation) check to discern the Simorgyan noble is disguised.

Incorporeal Form: The Simorgyan noble can use an action to become incorporeal when in humanoid form and on dry land. All objects carried by the Simorgyan noble also become incorporeal along with it. The Simorgyan noble remains incorporeal for 1 minute, or until it uses an action to return to physical form or change out of its humanoid form. The incorporeal state also ends if the Simorgyan noble comes into contact with salt water or is reduced to 0 hit points.

While in this incorporeal state, it gains the following traits:

- **Damage Resistances:** acid, cold, fire, lightning, poison, thunder; bludgeoning, piercing, and slashing damage from nonmagical attacks.

- **Incorporeal Movement:** The Simorgyan noble can move through other creatures and objects as if they were difficult terrain. It takes 5 (1d10) force damage if it ends its turn inside an object.

- **Sickening Touch:** The Simorgyan noble can use the Sickening Touch action.

Sea Tied: The Simorgyan noble has disadvantage on attack rolls, ability checks, and physical saving throws when in humanoid form and on dry land. If the Simorgyan noble is on a ship or otherwise surrounded by but not immersed in water then it does not suffer from this effect.

Spellcasting: The Simorgyan noble is a 5th-level spellcaster. Its spellcasting ability is Charisma (spell save DC 13, +5 to hit with spell attacks). The Simorgyan noble knows the following spells:

- Cantrips (at will): *blade ward, friends, light, shocking grasp, true strike*
- 1st level (4 slots): *charm person, fog cloud, shield*
- 2nd level (3 slots): *hold person, suggestion*
- 3rd level (2 slots): *lightning bolt*

ACTIONS

Multiattack (Humanoid or Hybrid Form Only): The Simorgyan noble makes two attacks, only one of which can be a bite.

Bite (Hunter Shark or Hybrid Form Only): *Melee Weapon Attack:* +3 to hit, reach 5 ft., one target. *Hit:* 10 (2d8 + 1) piercing damage.

Longsword (Humanoid or Hybrid Form Only): *Melee Weapon Attack:* +3 to hit, reach 5 ft., one target. *Hit:* 5 (1d8 + 1) slashing damage, or 6 (1d10 + 1) slashing damage if used with two hands.

Sickening Touch (Recharge 5-6) (Incorporeal Form Only): *Melee Weapon Attack:* +4 to hit, reach 5 ft., one creature. *Hit:* 9 (2d8) poison damage, and the target must succeed on a DC 11 Constitution saving throw, or become poisoned for 1 hour.

SIMORGYAN MANTA

Simorgyan mantas are denizens of legendary sunken Simorgya and are of unknown origin. They may be directly related to the drowned race of Simorgya or merely weird undersea creatures drawn to the inundated ruins of that lost kingdom. They resemble human-sized, leathery cloaks when viewed from afar. Up close, the toothy mouths located on the underside of their bodies and their bulbous, unblinking silver eyes are visible.

SIMORGYAN MANTA

Medium monstrosity, neutral evil

Armor Class: 14 (natural armor)

Hit Points: 26 (4d8 + 8)

Speed: 10 ft., fly 30 ft., swim 40 ft.

STR	DEX	CON	INT	WIS	CHR
18 (+4)	15 (+2)	14 (+2)	8 (-1)	10 (+0)	6 (-2)

Skills: Athletics +6, Stealth +4

Senses: blindsight 10 ft., passive Perception 10

Languages: understands Common but can't speak (understands Simorgyan but can't speak)

Challenge: 1 (200 XP)

Amphibious: The Simorgyan manta can breathe air and water.

False Appearance: While the Simorgyan manta remains motionless without its underside exposed, it is indistinguishable from a brown leather cloak.

Glide: The Simorgyan manta can fly up to 30 feet each round, but it must end its turn back on the ground. If it cannot land on solid ground at the end of its turn, it falls prone on the ground, suffering normal falling damage if applicable.

ACTIONS

Multiattack: The Simorgyan manta makes one bite attack, and if it is grappling a creature, the Simorgyan manta can also make one constrict attack against that creature.

Bite: *Melee Weapon Attack:* +6 to hit, reach 5 ft., one target. *Hit:* 8 (1d8 + 4) piercing damage, and if the creature is Medium or smaller, it is enveloped and grappled (escape DC 16). Until this grapple ends, the creature is restrained and the Simorgyan manta cannot envelop or bite another target. It has advantage on attack rolls to bite an enveloped victim.

Constrict: *Melee Weapon Attack:* +6 to hit, reach 5 ft., one target. *Hit:* 11 (2d6 + 4) bludgeoning damage.

SNOW SERPENT

Snow serpents are tremendous cold-climate snakes measuring up to 40 feet long and covered in white fur. With heads the size of an elk's, these warm-blooded serpents are ambush predators, preying on mountain goats, white bears, reindeer, and other large mammals that prowl the northern extremes. They supplement their diets with the occasional unwary human that enters their territory. Luckily, the snakes are usually only encountered in cold, desolate environments such as the Cold Waste, the Death Lands of Rime Isle, and high mountain ranges. Snow serpents possess violet-colored eyes and are venomous.

Unlike other snakes, snow serpents are armed with rows of shark-like teeth as well as venom-filled fangs to incapacitate and consume their prey. These fangs constantly leak a toxic mist and the snake can poison foes with its breath as well as its bite. Snow serpents are solitary hunters and typically encountered alone. However, during breeding season (late fall), up to a dozen snakes come together to breed and become highly aggressive.

SNOW SERPENT

Huge beast, unaligned

Armor Class: 13 (natural armor)

Hit Points: 68 (8d12 + 16)

Speed: 30 ft.

STR	DEX	CON	INT	WIS	CHR
19 (+4)	14 (+2)	14 (+2)	1 (-5)	10 (+0)	3 (-4)

Skills: Perception +2, Stealth +4

Damage Resistances: cold

Senses: blindsight 10 ft., passive Perception 12

Languages: —

Challenge: 2 (450 XP)

Snow Camouflage: The snow serpent has advantage on Dexterity (Stealth) checks made to hide in snowy or icy terrain.

ACTIONS

Bite: *Melee Weapon Attack:* +6 to hit, reach 10 ft., one target. *Hit:* 11 (2d6 + 4) piercing damage, and the target must make a DC 12 Constitution saving throw, taking 10 (3d6) poison damage on a failed save, or half as much damage on a successful one.

Poison Breath (Recharge 5-6): The snow serpent exhales poison breath in a 10-foot cone. Each creature in that area must make a DC 12 Constitution saving throw, taking 7 (2d6) poison damage and becoming poisoned for 1 hour on a failed save, or half as much damage and does not become poisoned on a successful one.

STATUE OF THE DEVOURERS

When the Devourers attempted to infiltrate Lankhmar through the Plaza of Dark Delights, either they brought with them a marvelous statue to guard their Bazaar of the Bizarre, or the statue was itself a Devourer. If Sheelba of the Eyeless Face or Ningauble of the Seven Eyes knows the truth, they are not telling. In either event, this statue ap-

peared to be a tall, black iron statue, slightly larger than human, with a visage that showed both dire threat and a melancholy brooding. The statue bore a two-handed sword.

Each statue of the Devourers is cloaked in a magical illusion making it appear to be a member of the invaded dimension's native species. The statue is quite personable in this mundane form and is typically encountered as the proprietor of a shop or marketplace offering wondrous items for sale.

STATUE OF THE DEVOURERS

Medium construct, lawful evil

Armor Class: 18 (natural armor)

Hit Points: 52 (8d8 + 16)

Speed: 30 ft.

STR	DEX	CON	INT	WIS	CHR
16 (+3)	12 (+1)	15 (+2)	10 (+0)	10 (+0)	12 (+1)

Skills: Deception +3, Persuasion +3

MASTER OR SERVANT?

The Devourers—an extradimensional race dedicated to cornering the cosmos' markets and enslaving its inhabitants with materialistic compulsions—appear in the story "The Bazaar of the Bizarre." While both the Gray Mouser and Fafhrd confront and defeat the Devourers' incursion into Nehwon, the identity of the foe they face is never undisputedly revealed. Was this animated statue a Devourer or just one of its agents?

The entry in this work assumes that the statue the duo defeated was a servant of the Devourers. As Ningauble explains in the story, "...the Devourers must occupy all their cunning in perfecting their methods of selling and so have not an instant to spare in considering the worth of what they sell." It stands to reason that the Devourers are so intent on enslaving the universe and besting each other that they leave the day-to-day business of selling irresistible trash to underlings. In this case, created automatons designed to sell and protect their cosmic marketplaces.

Game Masters are free to make their own assumptions for their individual campaigns. If the statue of the Devourers presented herein is just an agent of those extradimensional merchants, what is their true form and what powers might they possess?

Damage Resistances: bludgeoning, piercing, and slashing from nonmagical attacks that aren't adamantine

Senses: darkvision 60 ft., passive Perception 10

Languages: any one language (any one language)

Challenge: 4 (1,100 XP)

Illusory Appearance: The statue of the Devourers covers itself and anything it is wearing or carrying with a magical illusion that makes it look like another creature of its general size and humanoid shape. The illusion ends if the statue of the Devourers is destroyed.

The changes wrought by this effect fail to hold up to physical inspection. For example, the statue of the Devourers could appear to have soft flesh, but anyone touching it would feel cold iron. Otherwise, a creature must take an action to visually inspect the illusion and succeed on a DC 20 Intelligence (Investigation) check to discern the statue of the Devourers is disguised.

Unexpected Attack Vulnerability: In addition to having advantage as normal, any creature the statue of the Devourers cannot see doubles its proficiency bonus when attacking the statue.

ACTIONS

Multiattack: The statute of the Devourers makes two greatsword attacks.

Greatsword: *Melee Weapon Attack:* +5 to hit, reach 5 ft., one target. *Hit:* 10 (2d6 + 3) slashing damage.

REACTIONS

Reflect Missile: The statue of the Devourers can reflect a ranged attack directed at it if the missile is at least partially composed of metal (arrow, bolt, sling bullet, throwing knife, etc.). The statue ignores the attack roll unless it is a critical hit, and immediately sends the missile back at the original attacker. The statue of the Devourers makes a ranged attack with a +3 modifier against the attacker. Range penalties, cover, etc. modify the reflected missile attack as normal. The statue of the Devourers cannot reflect the original ranged attack if it achieved a critical hit on its attack roll.

WAR CAT

According to certain wise women and learned scholars, each type of animal has a governing body of 13 members. The War Cats are the bloodthirsty Inner Circle governing body of felines, known to rumor and legend, and hinted at within certain cave drawings found north of the Cold Waste and south of Quarmall. They appear as solid black cats, slender and long-legged like cheetahs, but with the mass of lions or tigers, and nearly as tall at the shoulder as a horse. Their heads are somewhat small for their size, but their needle-like fangs are like faintly green ice and their eyes like frozen emeralds.

There are always 13 War Cats. If one is struck down, it is replaced from the ranks of lesser felines.

WAR CAT

Large fey, chaotic neutral

Armor Class: 12

Hit Points: 60 (8d10 + 16)

Speed: 40 ft.

STR	DEX	CON	INT	WIS	CHR
19 (+4)	14 (+2)	15 (+2)	8 (-1)	13 (+1)	8 (-1)

Skills: Perception +3, Stealth +4

Senses: darkvision 60 ft., passive Perception 13

Languages: Sylvan, understands Common but can't speak it (Cat, understands Low Lankhmarese but can't speak it)

Challenge: 2 (450 XP)

Keen Smell: The War Cat has advantage on Wisdom (Perception) checks that rely on smell.

Pounce: If the War Cat moves at least 20 feet straight toward a creature and then hits it with a claw attack on the same turn, that target must succeed on a DC 14 Strength saving throw or be knocked prone. If the target is prone, the War Cat can make one bite attack against it as a bonus action.

ACTIONS

Bite: *Melee Weapon Attack:* +6 to hit, reach 5 ft., one target. *Hit:* 10 (1d12 + 4) piercing damage.

Claw: *Melee Weapon Attack:* +6 to hit, reach 5 ft., one target. *Hit:* 9 (1d10 + 4) slashing damage.

The tales of Fafhrd and the Gray Mouser wouldn't be "sword & sorcery" without wizardly adversaries and weird artifacts to challenge and confound them. This section delves into the arcane objects and magical practices of Nehwon, providing Game Masters with new spells and magical items to incorporate into their campaigns.

RANGER SPELLS

1st Level
Elude

SORCERER SPELLS

1st Level
Elude

Mouse's Contagion

2nd Level
The Snow Women's Icy Restraint

3rd Level
Hristomilo's Strangling Fog

WARLOCK SPELLS

1st Level
Mouse's Contagion

2nd Level
Mouse's Pain Transference

9th Level
Sheelba of the Eyeless Face's Great Spell

WIZARD SPELLS

1st Level
Elude

Mouse's Contagion

2nd Level
Mouse's Pain Transference

3rd Level
Hristomilo's Strangling Fog

9th Level
Sheelba of the Eyeless Face's Great Spell

NEW SPELL DESCRIPTIONS

The following spells are arranged in alphabetical order for ease of reference.

ELUDE

1st-level illusion

Casting Time: 1 action
Range: Touch
Components: V, S
Duration: 1 hour

You touch a creature and obscure the scent and signs of its passage through an area, making it difficult for pursuers to track it by sight or scent. While this spell is in effect, all Wisdom (Survival) checks to track the target and Wisdom (Perception) checks to detect its scent have disadvantage. Ability checks made to hear the target or to see its physical form are unaffected.

At Higher Levels: When you cast this spell using a spell slot of 2nd level or higher, you obscure the scent and passage of one additional creature for each slot level above 1st. For example, a 3rd-level spell slot masks the scent and tracks of a total of three subjects.

HRISTOMILO'S STRANGLING FOG

3rd-level conjuration

Casting Time: 1 action
Range: 90 feet
Components: V, S, M (an alembic containing black ink)
Duration: Concentration, up to 1 minute

Inky black strands of mist fill a 20-foot square in a space you can see within range. When a creature enters the affected area or starts its turn there, the creature must succeed on a Constitution saving throw or take 2d6 bludgeoning damage as the fog strangles them. Additionally, the creature is restrained by the magical smoke until the spell ends. A creature that starts its turn in the area and is already restrained by the smoke takes 2d6 bludgeoning damage.

A creature restrained by the strangling fog can use its action to make a Strength or Dexterity check (its choice) against your spell DC. It frees itself on a success.

MOUSE'S CONTAGION

1st-level necromancy

Casting Time: 10 minutes
Range: Special
Components: V, S, M (a poppet depicting the spell's target)
Duration: 24 hours

You engage in a prolonged spellcasting that afflicts a single target with a debilitating sickness. To affect a creature you must either be within 120 feet of it or you must possess a piece of the creature's body such as a fingernail paring, a lock of hair, a drop of blood, etc. If you have a piece of the target's body, you can cast the spell on that creature provided it is on the same plane of existence as you. The targeted creature must succeed on a Constitution saving throw or gain one level of exhaustion for 24 hours as sickness ravages their body. This level of exhaustion cannot be recovered via normal rest during the 24 hours the spell is in effect, but *lesser restoration* removes it before that time.

At Higher Levels: When you cast this spell using a spell slot of 2nd level or higher, the spell's duration is extended by an additional 24 hours for each slot level above 1st. The target is allowed another Constitution saving throw every 24 hours. If successful, the target escapes the spell's effects and can recover from exhaustion normally. Otherwise, they gain another exhaustion level as the contagion worsens.

MOUSE'S PAIN TRANSFERENCE

2nd-level abjuration

Casting Time: 1 action
Range: Self
Components: V, S
Duration: Concentration, up to 1 minute

This spell allows the caster to endure pain and suffering, all the while storing a portion of that harm to unleash upon another. While this spell is in effect, the caster gains resistance to acid damage, fire damage, and bludgeoning, piercing, and slashing damage from nonmagical attacks. The caster takes half damage from those attacks, storing the other half in a magical "battery." At any time during the spell's duration, the caster can unleash that stored damage at a single target within 10 feet. The target of this stored suffering takes necrotic damage equal to the amount of damage in the battery, or half as much with a successful Constitution saving throw.

For example, the caster is struck three times while this spell is in effect, suffering 10 nonmagical slashing damage, 5 thunder damage, and 6 nonmagical piercing damage. The caster takes 13 damage (5 slashing, 5 thunder, and 3 piercing) and stores 8 damage in the "battery" (5 slashing and 3 piercing). At any time thereafter until the spell ends, the caster could use an action to cause a single target within range to take 8 necrotic damage, or 4 necrotic damage with a successful Constitution saving throw.

Alternately, the caster can designate another person to serve as a conduit for this pain transference. The chosen conduit must be willing to act as the caster's proxy and be within 60 feet of the caster. The caster and conduit must be able to make eye contact with one another. If these conditions are met, the conduit serves as the pain transference's point of origin when the stored suffering is unleashed. If the conduit it physically touching the target of the spell when the transference occurs, the target has disadvantage on its Constitution saving throw.

The caster must make concentration checks as normal each time they suffer injury while maintaining this spell. However, if the injury comes from a damage type to which the spell grants resistance (acid or fire; bludgeoning, piercing, or slashing from nonmagical attacks), the caster has advantage on the concentration check. All stored damage is lost if the caster loses concentration on the spell for any reason or the spell's duration elapses.

SHEELBA OF THE EYELESS FACE'S GREAT SPELL

9th-level enchantment

Casting Time: 10 minutes
Range: 60 feet
Components: V, S
Duration: Instantaneous

You create a blast of powerful magic capable of slaying creatures outright, rendering them into dust. Creatures within 20 feet of a point you choose within range are affected in ascending order of their current hit points. A number of creatures whose current hit point total equals up to 100 hit points are affected.

Starting with the creature that has the lowest current hit points, each creature affected by this spell dies and becomes a pile of gray ashes. Subtract each creature's hit points from the total before moving on to the creature with the next lowest hit points. A creature's hit points must be equal to or less than the remaining total for that creature to be affected.

Undead and constructs aren't affected by this spell.

This spell was given to the Gray Mouser by his wizardly mentor, Sheelba of the Eyeless Face. It didn't go as the Mouser expected when he finally got his opportunity to cast it.

THE SNOW WOMEN'S ICY RESTRAINT

2nd-level conjuration

Casting Time: 1 action
Range: 60 feet
Components: V, S, M (an icicle)
Duration: Concentration, up to 1 minute

You conjure a mass of frigid cold that fills a 20-foot cube at a point of your choosing within range. The bone-numbing cold freezes muscles for the duration, impeding movement and causing frostbite. When a creature enters the affected area or starts its turn there, it must succeed on a Strength saving throw or become restrained. Additionally, a creature starting its turn in the affected area takes 2d6 cold damage.

A creature restrained by the frigid conditions can use its action to make a Strength or Dexterity check (its choice) against your spell DC. It frees itself on a success.

ARCANE ARTIFACTS

Nehwon is a magically-poor world in comparison to some other fantasy realms. Few magical items have ever been created or discovered, and most of those are in the possession of archmages and other powerful magic-workers. On rare occasions, these worthies may lend these objects to their agents—so long as it benefits themselves—but they more often covet and squirrel away these potent wonders.

Despite this, a few magical trinkets have been encountered by the dubious heroes who stride the lands of Nehwon, while other are hinted about in the writings of Skrith of the Scrolls. These are detailed below.

BLINDFOLD OF TRUE SEEING

Wondrous item, legendary

This strand of cloth resembles darkened cobwebs more than a strip of fabric. When worn, you can use an action to activate the blindfold's magic and gain truesight out to 60 feet for 10 minutes. The blindfold has 1d3 uses when found. When the last use has expired, Sheelba of the Eyeless Face or one of her agents appears briefly at the owner's location and snatches away the item, then vanishes with it.

CLOAK OF INVSIBILITY

Although little more than a tattered and shopworn, yard-long scrap of fabric rather than a true cloak, this object functions exactly as described in the core rules.

CUIRASS OF MINGSWARD

Armor (medium), very rare

Crafted by Mingsward the famed armorer of the Eastern Lands, this cuirass is of such cunning design that it fits the wearer like a second skin, allowing it to be worn under normal clothing without leaving so much as a bulge. It acts like breastplate armor when worn. In addition, you gain a +2 bonus to your AC when wearing the *cuirass of Mingsward*.

DART OF EMOTIONS

Weapon (dart), rare

This silver dart charms a humanoid creature struck by it, making them feel beholden to and infatuated with the weapon's wielder. The dart can either be thrown by hand (range 20/60 ft.) or discharged from a hand crossbow (range 30/120 ft.). The dart grants a +1 bonus to ranged attack rolls and does 1 point of piercing damage. It is considered a magical attack for purposes of damage resistance and immunity.

ATTUNEMENT AND ARCHMAGES

The archmages Sheelba of the Eyeless Face and Ningauble of the Seven Eyes are incredibly powerful wizards and may in fact be more god than sorcerer. This allows them to occasionally overturn normal magical rules. If either of the two directly presents an individual with a magical item that normally requires attunement, the receiver is considered automatically attuned to the object provided they meet any requirements necessary for attunement. This explains why Fafhrd was able to use the *cloak of invisibility* immediately before entering the Bazaar of the Bizarre and facing off against the Devourers' assault on Nehwon.

A humanoid successfully struck by the dart must make a DC 20 Wisdom saving throw. On a failed save, the target is charmed by the dart's wielder. This condition lasts until magically counteracted or the dart is removed from the target's flesh. The victim can also attempt another saving throw every 24 hours to resist the dart's enchantment and break the charmed condition.

The dart can be removed from a victim with a successful DC 15 Strength check. The dart's victim cannot attempt to remove the dart and will physically resist all attempts by others to pluck it from its flesh.

ELIXIR OF GHOSTS

Potion, rare

This elixir is deep purple in color and has a sickeningly sweet odor. It is salty like blood to the taste. When consumed, it sends the drinker's soul into the Ethereal Plane, leaving its body inert and defenseless on the Material Plane. This elixir was first used by a nameless old man who employed it to feed the ghost hounds (q.v.) that sought to claim his soul.

When consumed, the target's body becomes inert while its soul moves to the Ethereal Plane. The drinker is treated as if under the effects of an *etherealness* spell for 1 hour.

The drinker's body is vulnerable to physical attacks while its soul is in the Ethereal Plane. Any harm done to the body is instantly felt by the ethereal soul. The drinker can return to its physical form as an action, prematurely ending the potion's effect if the body suffers harm.

GROIN-PIECE OF GORTCH

Wondrous item, legendary (requires attunement)

This metal and leather undergarment helps protect the wearer and can easily be worn under clothing without being noticed. The groin-piece grants a +3 bonus to AC.

HISVIN'S POTIONS

Potion, rare

Hisvin, the Grain Merchant of Lankhmar, was known to possess two types of potions that allowed him, his daughter, and their allies to travel freely between the worlds of Lankhmar Above and rat-controlled Lankhmar Below. One potion was white in coloration, the other black in hue. Each had a different effect when consumed.

The white potion acts as a *potion of growth*. The black potion has the same effects as a *potion of diminution*. Both are described in the core rules.

HRISTOMILO'S RING

Ring, rare (requires attunement)

This ring amplifies the link between a wizard and their familiar, increasing the distance the spellcaster can communicate, share senses, and cast magic via the magical companion. It appears as a fire-blackened brass ring with two tiny rubies resembling the eyes of a rat set into the band's exterior.

A wizard wearing the ring can expend spell slots to increase the range in which they can interact with their familiar. The range is increased by 100 feet per spell slot level beyond the usual 100-foot range. For example, a wizard expending a 3rd-level spell slot could communicate telepath-

ically, experience the world through the familiar's senses, and deliver a spell with a range of touch up to 400 feet away (100-foot base plus 300 feet for a 3rd-level spell slot).

Additionally, the wizard can use the link with the familiar to cast spells with a range greater than touch. These spells use the familiar's position when determining the spell's point of origin or if the target is in range as applicable. However, due to the imperfect nature of spellcasting at distance via a proxy, targets of the spell's effect have advantage on saving throws to minimize the spell's magic. Spells that require an attack roll by the caster have disadvantage but use the caster's attack modifier as normal.

WHERE'S *SCALPEL*, *CAT'S CLAW*, AND *GRAYWAND*?

Fans of Fafhrd and the Gray Mouser's adventures are undoubtedly familiar with the two heroes' weapons: Mouser's sword, *Scalpel*, and his dagger, *Cat's Claw*, as well as Fafhrd's broadsword, *Graywand*. There's nothing to indicate in the story that these weapons were anything extraordinary; the Twain's success in combat owes more to their own martial prowess than to enchanted weaponry.

However, these weapons are legendary due to their owners' renown and some GMs might desire to include them in their campaigns as rewards to be granted or mythic arms to be sought. With Nehwon's many connections to other worlds and the penchant of the Twain to run afoul of cosmic forces or suffer ill luck, it's no stretch of the imagination to suggest that these weapons ended up on some other world. Here are suggestions for magical versions of these famed blades for your campaign:

CAT'S CLAW
Weapon (dagger), rare (requires attunement)

This poignard is an extremely sharp and use-worn dagger with its handle wrapped in gray mouseskin. You gain a +1 bonus to attack and damage rolls made with this weapon. Once per day you can draw upon the dagger's magic to grant yourself advantage on a single attack roll. If you normally get multiple strikes with a single attack action, only the first attack roll has advantage.

GRAYWAND
Weapon (longsword), rare (requires attunement)

This blade is a well-balanced sword and seems meant to be wielded by a tall, strong owner. You gain a +1 bonus to attack and damage rolls made with this weapon. In addition, whenever you achieve a critical hit with the sword, you can reroll one damage die and take the best result.

SCALPEL
Weapon (longsword), rare (requires attunement)

This sword is remarkably well-balanced and light. Its blade is razor-sharp and never grows dull with normal use. The weapon is both a light and finesse weapon but lacks the versatile property typical for a longsword. You gain a +1 bonus to attack and damage rolls made with this weapon.

WAR CAT WHISTLE

Wondrous item, very rare

This object is a slim tin whistle said to have once been owned by a wise woman of the northern lands. It has a string of 13 undecipherable characters lining one side of it and the figure of a slender feline beast resting on its legs with head raised high on the other. When blown, the whistle produces a sound described as "the scream of a leopard, the snarl of a tiger, and the roaring of a lion commingled."

You can use an action to sound this whistle. Doing so calls 13 War Cats (q.v.) from their plane of existence who appear within 60 feet of you.

The War Cats return to their home plane after 1 hour, when reduced to 0 hit points, or when all enemies of catdom in the immediate vicinity have been slain. It is said that the *War Cat whistle* only works once in a lifetime for any particular individual or group of individuals (such as a party of adventurers). After this single use, the whistle produces only a shrill trilling when blown.

When summoned, the War Cats instantly attack whatever creature or creatures, beast or human, in the immediate area of the whistle they deem to be the biggest threat to felines. If none are present, the War Cats likely turn upon the whistle-blower unless that person is a lifelong ailurophile (GM's discretion). If no threat is present and they deem the whistle-blower unworthy of savaging, the War Cats immediately depart.

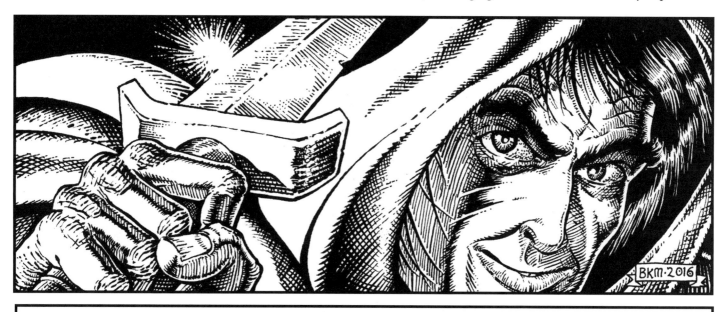

FIFTH EDITION FANTASY

Stand-alone, world-neutral adventure modules compatible with 5E. All print editions also include a code for free PDF edition. Look for them at your local game store or **www.goodman-games.com**!

Original Adventures Reincarnated are an homage to the origins of our hobby! Each volume contains high-quality scans from multiple printings of the original first edition adventure modules, plus commentary by gaming legends. Full fifth edition conversions are included, as well as brand new adventure material that adds new encounters and expands the original encounters.